THE SWEET

The Sweet is a glam rock band formed in 1968, London, England, UK that became famous in the early 1970s. Their best known line-up comprised lead vocalist Brian Connolly, bass player Steve Priest, guitarist Andy Scott, and drummer Mick Tucker. The group was originally called Sweetshop. The group had their first hit, "Funny Funny" in 1971, after teaming up with songwriters Nicky Chinn and Mike Chapman with record producer Phil Wainman. From '71 - '72, their musical style progressed from the Archies-like, bubblegum style of "Funny Funny," to a Who-influenced hard-rock style, enhanced with the striking use of high-pitched backing vocals.

The band first had success in the UK charts, with thirteen Top 20 hits during the '70s alone, "Block Buster!" (1973) topping the charts, followed by three consecutive # 2 hits, "Hell Raiser" (1973), "The Ballroom Blitz" (1973) and "Teenage Rampage" (1974). The band then developed a harder rock style, with their mid-career singles, including 1974's "Turn It Down", with "Fox on the Run" (1975) also having reached # 2 on the UK charts. They had even greater success in West Germany and other countries on the European mainland, having also gained popularity in the US with the top ten hits "Little Willy", "The Ballroom Blitz" and "Fox on the Run".

Sweet had their last Top 10 hit in 1978 with "Love Is Like Oxygen", before Connolly left the group in 1979 to start a solo career, the remaining members having continued as a trio until disbanding in 1981. From the mid-1980s, Scott, Connolly and Priest each played with their own versions of Sweet, before Connolly died in 1997 then Tucker in 2002. The two surviving members are still active in their versions of the band, Scott's being based in the UK, Priest's in the US.

Sweet's origins lay in British soul band Wainwright's Gentlemen, Mark Lay's history of that band stating that they formed c.1962, having been known at first as Unit 4. Founder members included Chris Wright (vocals), Jan Frewer (bass), with Jim Searle and Alfred Fripp on guitars. Phil Kenton then joined on drums, as the group changed its name to Wainwright's Gentlemen, due to there being another band known as Unit 4, performing in the Hayes, Harrow and Wembley area, having been managed by Frewer's father. By 1964 the group was playing in central London, including at the Saint Germain Club, on Poland Street.

In January of that year the band came fifth in a national beat group contest, the finals having been held at the Lyceum Strand, on 4 May 1964, with Highlights of the show being presented on BBC1 by Alan Freeman. Chris Wright left the line-up in late 1964, having been replaced by Ian Gillan, with vocalist Ann Cully having joined the group before Mick Tucker, from Ruislip, joined on drums, replacing Phil Kenton.

The band recorded a number of tracks, including a cover of the Coasters-the Hollies' hit "Ain't That Just Like Me", probably at Jackson Sound Studios in Rickmansworth. The track includes Gillan on vocals and Tucker on drums, which Jan Frewer believed to have been recorded in 1965. Gillan quit in May 1965 to join Episode Six, later forming Deep Purple, before Cully also departed, her replacement as vocalist, in late 1966, being Scots-born Brian Connolly, who'd moved to Harefield.

Tony Hall had joined on saxophone and vocals, before Fripp left, first being replaced on guitar by Gordon Fairminer then Frank Torpey, a schoolfriend of Tucker's who'd just left West London group The Tribe, aka The Dream. Torpey only lasted a few months, before in late 1967 Robin Box took his place.

Guitarist Searle, widely regarded as the most talented musically, then disappeared from the scene. Tucker and Connolly remained with Wainwright's Gentlemen until January 1968, when Tucker was replaced by Roger Hills, before the Gentlemen broke up, Hills and Box having joined White Plains, which later had a big hit with "My Baby Loves Lovin'".

In January 1968 Connolly and Tucker formed a new band, calling themselves The Sweetshop, recruiting bass guitarist and lead vocalist Steve Priest, from a local band called the Army, who'd previously played with another local band the Countdowns. Frank Torpey was again recruited to play guitar, the quartet having made its public debut at the Pavilion in Hemel Hempstead on 4 March 1968, soon developing a following on the pub circuit, which led to a contract with Fontana Records.

Another UK band then released a single under the same name Sweetshop, so the group changed their name to The Sweet, being managed by Paul Nicholas, who later went on to star in Hair. Nicholas worked with record producer Phil Wainman at Mellin Music Publishing, to whom he recommended the band. Their debut single "Slow Motion" (July 1968), produced by Wainman, and released on Fontana, failed to chart, which owing to its rarity, sells for hundreds of pounds when auctioned.

Sweet were then released from their recording contract, with Frank Torpey having departed. In his autobiography Are You Ready Steve, Priest said that Gordon Fairminer was approached to play for them when Torpey decided to leave Sweet, after a gig at Playhouse Theatre Walton-on-Thames, on 5 July 1969 but turned the offer down.

Guitarist Mick Stewart joined in 1969, who had some rock pedigree, having previously worked with The (Ealing) Redcaps and Simon Scott & The All-Nite Workers in the mid-1960s. In late 1965, that band became The Phil Wainman Set, when the future Sweet producer joined on drums, the group having cut some singles with Errol Dixon. In early 1966, Stewart left, later working with Johnny Kidd & The Pirates.

The Sweet then signed a new record contract, with EMI's Parlophone label, three bubblegum pop singles being released: "Lollipop Man" (September 1969), "All You'll Ever Get from Me" (January 1970), and a cover version of the Archies' "Get on the Line" (June 1970), all of which failed to chart. Stewart then quit, without being replaced for some time.

Connolly and Tucker then had a chance meeting with Wainman, who was now producing, and knew of two aspiring songwriters, Nicky Chinn and Mike Chapman, who were looking for a group to sing over some demos which they'd written together. Connolly, Priest and Tucker provided the vocals on a track called "Funny Funny," which featured Pip Williams on guitar, John Roberts on bass and Wainman on drums.

The latter began offering the track to recording companies, as the band held auditions for a replacement guitarist, having settled on Welsh-born Andy Scott, who'd been playing in the Scaffold, with Mike McCartney, Paul of The Beatles brother. As a member of the Elastic Band, he'd also played guitar on two singles for Decca, "Think of You Baby" and "Do Unto Others", having appeared on the band's lone album release, Expansions on Life, and on some recordings by the Scaffold. The group rehearsed for a few weeks, before Scott made his live debut with Sweet on 26 September 1970, at the Windsor Ballroom in Redcar.

At first The Sweet attempted to combine various musical influences, including the Monkees and 1960s bubblegum pop groups such as the Archies, with more heavy rock-oriented groups like the Who. The Sweet adopted the rich vocal harmony style of the Hollies, with distorted guitars and a heavy rhythm section, with the fusion of pop and hard rock remaining a trademark of Sweet's music, presaging the glam rock a few years down the line.

The Sweet's first album was issued on the budget label Music for Pleasure, as part of a compilation called Gimme Dat Ding, in December 1970. The Sweet had one side of the record, with the Pipkins, whose sole hit, "Gimme Dat Ding", gave the LP its name, having had the other. The Sweet's side was comprised of the A- and B-sides of the band's three Parlophone singles. Andy Scott appeared in the album cover shot, although he didn't play on any of the recordings.

The Sweet made their UK TV debut in December 1970, on a pop show called Lift Off, performing the song "Funny Funny". A management deal was signed with the songwriting team of Nicky Chinn and Mike Chapman, Phil Wainman having resumed his collaboration with Sweet, as executive producer. This management deal also included a worldwide (excluding North America), record contract with RCA Records, while in the United States and Canada, Bell Records issued the group's music until late 1973, followed by Capitol Records.

In March 1971 RCA issued "Funny Funny", written by Chinn and Chapman, which became the group's first international hit, climbing into the Top 20 on many of the world's charts. EMI then reissued their 1970 single "All You'll Ever Get from Me" (May 1971), which again failed to chart. Their next RCA release "Co-Co" (June 1971) went to # 2 in the U.K. but their follow up single, "Alexander Graham Bell" (October 1971), only reached #33. These tracks still featured session musicians, with the quartet providing only the vocals.

The Sweet's first full LP album, Funny How Sweet Co-Co Can Be, was released in November 1971, being a collection of the band's recent singles, with some new Chinn/Chapman tunes, including "Chop Chop" and "Tom Tom Turnaround," with pop covers, the Lovin' Spoonful's "Daydream" and the Supremes' "Reflections"amongst others. The album, recorded at Nova Studios in London, was produced by Phil Wainman and engineered by Richard Dodd and Eric Holland but wasn't a real contender on the charts. Their L.P.s' failure to match the success of their singles was a problem that affected the band throughout their career.

February 1972 saw the release of "Poppa Joe", which hit # 1 in Finland, having reached # 11 in the UK Singles Chart. Their next two singles of that year, "Little Willy" and "Wig-Wam Bam", both reached No. 4 in the UK, with "Little Willy" having climbed to No. 3 on the U.S. Billboard Hot 100 after a re-issue in 1973, becoming the group's biggest American hit.

Although "Wig-Wam Bam" remained largely true to the style of the Sweet's previous recordings, the vocals and guitars had a harder, more rock-oriented sound, mainly because it was the first Chinn-Chapman single on which only members of Sweet played. In January 1973 "Block Buster!" became the Sweet's first single to hit # 1 on the UK chart, remaining there for five consecutive weeks. After their next single "Hell Raiser," was released in May, having reached # 2 in the U.K., the Sweet's U.S. label, Bell, released the group's first American album The Sweet, in July 1973.

To promote their singles, the Sweet made many appearances on U.K. and European TV shows, including Top of the Pops and Supersonic. During one performance of "Block Buster!" on Top of the Pops, Priest provoked complaints, after he appeared wearing a German uniform, displaying a swastika armband. The band capitalised on the glam rock explosion, rivalling Gary Glitter, T. Rex, Queen, Slade, and Wizzard for outrageous stage clothing.

Despite the Sweet's success, the relationship with their management was becoming increasingly tense, as while they'd developed a large fan-base among teenagers, the Sweet weren't happy with their 'bubblegum' image. The group had always composed their own heavy-rock songs on the B-sides of their singles, contrasting with the bubblegum A-sides, which were composed by Chinn and Chapman.

The Sweet's live performances comprised B-sides and album tracks, with various medleys of rock 'n' roll classics, having avoided older 'novelty' hits including "Funny Funny" and "Poppa Joe". A 1973 performance at the Palace Theatre and Grand Hall in Kilmarnock, ended with the Sweet being bottled off stage, the disorder having been attributed by Steve Priest amongst others, to the Sweet's lipstick and eye-shadow look, but by others to the audience being unfamiliar with the concert set.

The 1999 CD release 'Live at the Rainbow 1973,' documented a live show from this period, with the incident having been immortalised in the hit "The Ballroom Blitz", released in September 1973. The Sweet's chart success continued, having been especially strong in the UK, Denmark, Germany, Sweden and Australia. At the end of 1973, the band's name evolved from "The Sweet" to "Sweet", the change being reflected in all of their releases from 1974 onward.

By 1974, Sweet had grown tired of the management team of Chinn and Chapman, who wrote the group's major hits, cultivating the band's glam rock image. The group and producer Phil Wainman, assisted by engineer Peter Coleman, recorded the album Sweet Fanny Adams, which was released in April 1974.

Sweet's technical proficiency was demonstrated for the first time on self-penned hard rock tracks, including "Sweet F.A." and "Set Me Free", having adopted a more conventional hard rock sound and appearance. Sweet Fanny Adams featured compressed, high-pitched backing vocal harmonies, which was a trend that continued on all of their albums.

During sessions for the album, Brian Connolly's throat was badly injured in a fight in Staines High Street, his ability to sing being severely limited. Priest and Scott filled in on lead vocals on the tracks "No You

Don't", "Into The Night" and "Restless", before Connolly, receiving treatment from a Harley Street specialist, managed to complete the album. The band didn't publicise the incident, having told the press that cancelled shows were due to Connolly having a throat infection.

No previous singles appeared on the album, with none having been released, except in Japan, New Zealand and Australia, where "Peppermint Twist/Rebel Rouser", apparently issued by their record company without their knowledge, topped the charts in the latter. Sweet Fanny Adams was Sweet's only non-compilation release to break the UK Albums Chart Top 40.

Sweet were invited by Pete Townshend to support the Who, who were playing at Charlton Athletic's football ground, The Valley, in June 1974 but Connolly's badly bruised throat prevented them from taking up the offer. Sweet had frequently cited the Who as being one of their main influences, having played a medley of their tracks in their live set for many years.

Their third album, Desolation Boulevard, was released later in 1974, six months after Sweet Fanny Adams, by which time producer Phil Wainman had moved on, the L.P. having been produced by Mike Chapman, being recorded in just six days, featuring a rawer "live" sound. One track, "The Man with the Golden Arm", written by Elmer Bernstein and Sylvia Fine for the 1955 Frank Sinatra movie of the same name, featured drummer Mick Tucker performing an 8 1/2 minute solo, which had been a staple of the band's live performance for years, although this wasn't included in the U.S. release.

The first single from the LP, the heavy-melodic "The Six Teens", released in July 1974, was a Top 10 hit in the U.K., being part of the amazing unbroken string of #1s in Denmark. However, the following single release, "Turn It Down", in November 1974, reached only # 41 on the U.K. chart and #2 in Denmark.

It received minimal airplay on UK radio, having been banned by some radio stations because of its lyrical content - "God-awful sound" and "For God sakes, turn it down" - which were deemed "unsuitable for family listening." The band resumed playing live shows almost six full months after Connolly's throat injury, with band and critics noting a rougher edge to his voice and a reduced range. The album featured a group composition, "Fox On The Run", which was to be re-recorded months later.

The U.S. version of Desolation Boulevard was different from the U.K. version, having included several songs from Sweet Fanny Adams, as well as the "Ballroom Blitz" and "Fox on the Run" singles, both of which hit #5 in the US. Side one of the album comprised all Chapman-Chinn penned songs, while side two featured songs written and produced by Sweet.

In 1975 Sweet went back into the studio, to re-arrange and record a more pop-oriented version of the track "Fox on the Run". Their first self-written and produced single, "Fox on the Run" was released worldwide in March 1975, becoming their biggest selling hit, reaching # 1 in Germany, Denmark, and South Africa, # 2 in the United Kingdom, Ireland, Norway and the Netherlands and # 3 in Austria and Switzerland.

In Australia it not only topped the charts, but became the biggest selling single of that year, having reached # 2 in Canada and # 5 in the U.S. The release of the track marked the end of the formal Chinn-

Chapman working relationship, the band stressing that it was fully self-sufficient as writers and producers.

The following single release, in July 1975, "Action", reached # 15 in the UK, as Sweet spent the latter half of 1975 in Musicland Studios in Munich, Germany, where they recorded the Give Us A Wink album with German sound engineer Reinhold Mack, who later recorded with Electric Light Orchestra and co-produced Queen. The new album release was deferred until 1976, to avoid damaging the chart success of Desolation Boulevard, which reached # 25 in the US and # 5 in Canada.

With Give Us a Wink being held over, in November RCA issued a double album in Europe, Strung Up, which comprised a live disc, recorded in London in December 1973, with the other disc compiling previously released single tracks plus an unused track by Chinn and Chapman, "I Wanna Be Committed". At the end of '75, Andy Scott released his first solo single, "Lady Starlight" b/w "Where D'Ya Go", with Tucker having played drums on both tracks.

In January 1976 Sweet released the single "The Lies In Your Eyes", which made the Top 10 in Germany, Denmark, Finland, Sweden, the Netherlands, and Australia, but only reached No. 35 on the U.K. charts. Give Us A Wink, was released in March 1976, with the third single from the album, "4th Of July", having been issued in Australia.

Sweet tried to build on their growing popularity in America, with a schedule of more than fifty headline concert dates, with the band's set promoting the US version of Desolation Boulevard plus the new US hit single "Action", although Give Us A Wink's release was imminent. During an appearance at Santa Monica Civic Auditorium in California on 24 March, Sweet played "All Right Now" with Ritchie Blackmore, to mark the death of Free guitarist Paul Kossoff, who was to have supported Sweet with his band, Back Street Crawler. Following the end of the US tour, the band went on to Scandinavia and Germany, also having spent a week at the Who's Ramport Studios in Battersea, demoing material for a new album, before abandoning that project and playing eight dates in Japan.

Sweet then wrote and recorded new material at Kingsway Recorders and Audio International London studios for their next album, between October 1976 and January 1977. An advance single from the album, "Lost Angels", was only a hit in Germany, Austria and Sweden, before their new album, Off the Record, was released in April.

With the next single from the album, "Fever of Love", the group were heading in a more Europop hard rock direction, again charting in Germany, Austria and Sweden, and reaching # 10 in South Africa. Sweet worked with Give Us A Wink engineer Louis Austin, on the L.P., who later engineered Def Leppard's On Through The Night, début album in 1980. Sweet didn't play any live dates in support of the album, not having performed a single concert during the whole of 1977.

Sweet left RCA in 1977, signing a new deal with Polydor, which didn't come into force until later in the year, their manager David Walker, from Handle Artists, having negotiated the move, which was reputed to be worth c. £750,000. Capitol had issued Sweet's albums since 1974 in the United States, Canada and Japan, having continued to do so through 1980.

In their first Polydor album, Level Headed, issued during January 1978, featuring the single "Love Is Like Oxygen", Sweet experimented by combining rock and classical sounds "a-la clavesin", an approach similar to that of Electric Light Orchestra. Mainly recorded during 1977, at Château d'Hérouville near Paris, France and Clearwell Castle, in the Forest Of Dean, UK, the L.P. represented a new musical direction, with its Led Zeppelin influenced rock style, interspersed with ballads accompanied by a 30-piece orchestra. The ballad, "Lettres D'Amour", featured a duet between Connolly and Stevie Lange, who emerged as lead singer of the group Night in 1979.

Sweet then undertook a short European and Scandinavian tour, followed by a single British concert at London's Hammersmith Odeon on 24 February 1978, having added session and touring musicians, keyboardist Gary Moberley and guitarist Nico Ramsden. However, "Love Is Like Oxygen", released in January 1978, was their last U.K., U.S. and German Top 10 hit, with Scott having been nominated for an Ivor Novello Award for co-composing the song. One more single from the album, "California Nights", issued in May 1978, featuring Steve Priest as the lead vocalist, reached # 23 on the German charts.

Between March and May 1978, Sweet toured the US extensively, as a support act for Bob Seger and the Silver Bullet Band. The tour included a disastrous date in Birmingham, Alabama on 3 May, during which visiting Capitol Records executives in the audience saw Brian Connolly give a drunken and incoherent performance that ended early in the set with his collapse on stage, leaving the rest of the group to play on without him. The band then returned briefly to Britain, resuming the second leg of their US tour in late May, supporting other acts, including Foghat and Alice Cooper, before finishing the tour in early July 1978, with Brian's alcoholism steadily becoming a greater issue.

In late October, having spent more time at Clearwell Castle to write for their next album, Sweet arrived at The Town House studio in Shepherds Bush, London to complete and record, Cut Above the Rest, released in April 1979. As a last-ditch effort, the group had arranged for Connolly's long-time friend and fellow founding member, Mick Tucker, to go into the studio without Andy Scott as producer.

A number of tracks were recorded featuring Connolly on vocals but these efforts were deemed unsatisfactory, with Brian's being erased from the ensuing album, who then left the band. On 23 February 1979, Brian Connolly's departure from Sweet was announced by manager David Walker, Connolly having been said to be pursuing a solo career, with an interest in recording country rock.

Sweet continued as a trio, Steve Priest and Andy Scott handling lead vocals, with Mick Tucker still on drums, their first single release being "Call Me". Guest keyboard player Gary Moberley continued to join the group on stage and guitarist Ray McRiner joined their touring line-up in 1979. They embarked on a tour with Journey in the eastern United States and Cheap Trick in Texas in the spring and summer of '79, to support their album Cut Above The Rest, which was released in April 1979.

McRiner contributed the songs "Too Much Talking" and "Give The Lady Some Respect" to the next Sweet album, Waters Edge, issued in August 1980, which was recorded in Canada. In the US, Waters Edge was titled Sweet VI, featuring the singles "Sixties Man" and "Give The Lady Some Respect". Tragedy befell Mick Tucker when his wife Pauline drowned in the bath at their home, on 26 December 1979. The band then withdrew from live work for the whole of 1980.

One more studio album, Identity Crisis, was recorded during 1980–81, only being released in West Germany and Mexico. Sweet went on a short tour of the UK, performing their last live show at Glasgow University, on 20 March 1981. Steve Priest then returned to the United States, where he'd been living since late 1979, having soon remarried there. When Polydor released Identity Crisis in October 1982, the original Sweet had been disbanded for almost a year.

Andy Scott and Mick Tucker re-formed their own version of Sweet with Paul Mario Day, ex-Iron Maiden, More, Wildfire, on lead vocals, Phil Lanzon, ex-Grand Prix, on keyboards and Mal McNulty on bass. The band performed at the Marquee Club in London during February 1986, with the shows being recorded then released a few years later, bolstered by four new studio tracks, including a cover of the Motown standard "Reach Out I'll Be There".

This line-up toured Australian and New Zealand pubs and clubs for more than three months in 1985, followed by a similar period in early 1986. Singer Paul Mario Day married the band's Australian tour guide, relocating downunder. He continued to perform with Sweet, commuting back and forth to Europe for the group's tours, until this proved to be too tiresome, departing in late 1988.

As McNulty moved into the front man spot, Jeff Brown came in to take over on bass early in 1989. Phil Lanzon also transferred back and forth between Sweet and Uriah Heep during 1986-1988, before Heep's schedule grew too busy. Malcolm Pearson, followed by Ian Gibbons, who'd played with both The Kinks and The Records, both filled in for Lanzon, until Steve Mann, ex-Liar, Lionheart, McAuley Schenker Group, joined in December 1989.

Tucker departed after a show in Lochau, Austria on 5 May 1991, later having been diagnosed with a rare form of leukaemia. Three drummers, Andy Hoyler, Bobby Andersen and Bruce Bisland, ex-Weapon, Wildfire, Praying Mantis, filled-in, before the German, Bodo Schopf, ex-McAuley Schenker Group, took over.

The group recorded an album during this period, simply titled 'A', but before they embarked on the supporting tour for 'A' in 1992, Bodo left, with Bisland having returned as permanent percussionist. Scott changed the band's name to 'Andy Scott's Sweet' after Tucker's departure then truncated it to simply 'The Sweet', after Tucker's death in 2002.

Mal McNulty departed as vocalist in 1994, though he returned briefly that year to fill in for Jeff Brown on bass then again in 1995 as lead singer for a few dates, while Rocky Newton filled-in on bass. Sweet's former keyboard men Gary Moberley and Ian Gibbons also substituted with the group that year, as did Chris Goulstone, with Chad Brown, ex-Lionheart, no relation to Jeff, acting as their new front man. Glitz Blitz and Hitz, a new studio album of re-recorded Sweet hits, was released during this period.

In 1996 Mann left to take a job in TV, with Gibbons having come back for a short time before Steve Grant, ex-The Animals, became their permanent keyboardist. When Chad Brown quit in 1998, after developing a throat infection, Jeff Brown took on lead vocals and bass duties, with the band's line-up stabilizing for the next five years.

The mid-2000s then brought further confusing shake-ups and rotations, with Tony O'Hora, ex-Onslaught, Praying Mantis, replacing Brown as lead vocalist in 2003, before Ian Gibbons came back for a third stint as fill-in keyboardist in June 2005, for a gig in the Faroe Islands. O'Hora quit to take a teaching job in late 2005, with Grant then moving from keyboards to lead vocals and bass, as Phil Lanzon returned on keyboards for a tour of Russia and Germany in October/November.

Mark Thompson Smith, ex-Praying Mantis, joined as vocalist in November 2005 for some Swedish gigs, while Jo Burt, ex-Black Sabbath, was temporary bass player. Tony Mills, ex-Shy, was slated to be Sweet's new lead singer in early 2006 but failed to work out, leaving after six shows in Denmark. O'Hora then came back as fill in front man, with Grant having another turn as the singer/bassist, as Steve Mann deputized on keyboards, until the group finally got a new permanent front man, when Peter Lincoln, ex-Sailor, arrived in July 2006. The line-up then comprised Scott, Bisland, Grant and Lincoln.

Scott produced the Suzi Quatro album Back to the Drive, released in February 2006 then in March 2006, his band's album Sweetlife was released in the U.S. In 2007 the group played in Germany, Belgium, Austria and Italy, with the band also having played in Porto Alegre and Curitiba, Brazil, in May of that year, their only South American shows on the 'Sweet Fanny Adams Tour'.

The band toured again in March 2008, under the name 'Sweet Fanny Adams Revisited Tour'. In May and June, Scott's Sweet were part of the "Glitz Blitz & 70s Hitz" tour of the UK, alongside The Rubettes and Showaddywaddy. In March and April 2010, Scott missed a couple of gigs due to ill health, so Martin Mickels stood in, Scott later revealing that he'd been diagnosed with prostate cancer, being treated at Bristol Royal Infirmary. After a course of treatment and rest, he was back to full touring fitness, as the band played at venues in Europe then back at Bilston in October of that year.

In March 2011 there was a short tour of Australia, including the Regal Theatre - Perth, and Clipsal 500, Adelaide, with the Doobie Brothers. Tony O'Hora came back into the group that year as keyboardist, after Grant departed then in March 2012 the band released a new album, New York Connection. Recorded in England, it comprised 11 cover versions, including the 2011 single "Join Together", with one revamped original recording; the 1972 B-side "New York Connection".

All the covers either featured 'bits and pieces' of Sweet hits or other artist songs, including a "new version of the Ramones Blitzkrieg Bop, which shared space with samples from 'Ballroom Blitz,' and a take on Hello's New York Groove, made famous in the US by Ace Frehley, featured a sample from Jay-Z's Empire State Of Mind, along with other Sweet references."

On the eve of their March 2012 "Join Together" tour of Australia, the band played acoustic versions of three tracks, "New York Groove-Empire State of Mind", "Blockbuster" and "Peppermint Twist", in front of a live audience at ABC Radio Studios in East Perth. Shows in Perth, Adelaide, Hobart, Geelong, Melbourne and Sydney then featured tracks from their new album for the first time.

Paul Manzi joined Sweet on their 2014 Australian tour, replacing Tony O'Hora, who was absent for personal reasons. Manzi played guitar, keyboard and performed lead vocals on "Set Me Free" and "AC-DC," as the band gave shows in regional centres, including outback Western Australia, Darwin and far-north Queensland, New South Wales and Victoria during February and March.

The group, with O'Hora back in their ranks, returned to Australia in September 2014, as the headlining act for "Rock The Boat 4", a cruise aboard the ship Rhapsody of the Seas, which departed Sydney, having taken in New Caledonia and Vanuatu. The band played two gigs and various members guested with Australian veteran performers, including Brian Cadd and Russell Morris, members of AC/DC, The Angels, Rose Tattoo and Skyhooks.

In June 2015 it was announced that the band were embarking on an extensive tour of the UK in late 2015, which would probably be their last. For the 2015 summer tour dates, Paul Manzi returned to substitute for Peter Lincoln, who left the online message for fans: "There have been a few rumours going around this weekend, so . . . just to say that I am alive and well! The short explanation for my absence is that I need to rest my voice for a few weeks. We are lucky that our good friend Paul Manzi is able to step in, and Tony knows the role of bass player/singer, so the shows can go ahead, and they will be great! I look forward to being back on stage very soon."

Pete Lincoln duly resumed his role in the band, as they continued on an extensive series of live dates, known as the "Finale" tour in Germany. In 2017, after Andy took part in a successful Australian visit with Suzi Quatro and Don Powell, in the side outfit known as QSP, Sweet was again booked for an extensive European tour.

In 1984 Brian Connolly formed a new version of the Sweet, without any of the other original members. Despite his recurring ill health, Connolly toured the UK and Europe with his band, "Brian Connolly's Sweet", which was then renamed "New Sweet". His most successful concerts were in West Germany, before and after reunification.

During 1987, Connolly met up again with Frank Torpey, who later stated in interviews that Connolly was trying to get a German recording deal. The two got on very well, so Torpey later invited Connolly to go into the recording studio with him, as an informal project. After much trepidation, Connolly turned up, with the track "Sharontina" being recorded, which wasn't released until 1998, when it appeared on Frank Torpey's album Sweeter.

By July 1990, plans had been made for Connolly and his band to tour Australia in November, but during the long flight to Australia, Brian's health suffered, being hospitalised in Adelaide Hospital, with dehydration and related problems. The rest of the band played a show in Adelaide without him, before Connolly was released from hospital, joining them in Melbourne for a gig at the Pier Hotel, in Frankston.

Following several other shows, including one at the Dingley Powerhouse, Connolly and his band played a final date at Melbourne's Greek Theatre. Brian's health prevented the tour from being extended, with some of the planned dates having to be abandoned. Connolly went back to England then his band appeared on The Bob Downe Christmas show, on 18 December 1990.

During the early 1990s, Brian played the European "oldies" circuit and occasional outdoor festivals in Europe with his group. On 22 March 1992, a heavy duty tape recorder was stolen from the band's van, whilst at a gig in the Bristol Hippodrome with Mud, which contained demos of four new songs, totaling about 20 mixes.

Legal problems were ongoing, over the use of the Sweet name, between Connolly and Andy Scott, with both parties having agreed to distinguish their group's names to help promoters and fans. The New Sweet went back to being called Brian Connolly's Sweet and Andy Scott's version became Andy Scott's Sweet.

In 1994 Brian and his band played in Dubai, appearing at the Galleria Theatre, Hyatt Regency, having also performed in Bahrain. By this time Connolly had smoothed over his differences with Steve Priest and Mick Tucker, having been invited to the wedding of Priest's eldest daughter, Lisa, when Priest and Connolly performed together at the private function, for which Priest had flown back to England. In 1995 Brian released a new album entitled Let's Go and his partner Jean, whom he'd met a few years earlier, gave birth to a son. Connolly also performed in Switzerland that year.

On 2 November 1996, British TV Network Channel 4 aired the programme "Don't Leave Me This Way", which examined Brian's time as a pop star with the Sweet, their decline in popularity, and its impact on Connolly and the other band members. The show covered Brian's ill health but also stated that he was continuing with his concert dates at Butlins, where Connolly and his band had appeared a number of times on tour, during the early 1990s. Brian's final concert was at the Bristol Hippodrome on 5 December 1996, with Slade II and John Rossall's Glitter Band Experience.

In January 2008 Steve Priest assembled his own version of the Sweet in Los Angeles, having enlisted guitarist Stuart Smith, with L.A. native Richie Onori, Smith's bandmate in Heaven & Earth, being brought in on drums. Keyboards were played by ex-Crow and World Classic Rockers alumni Stevie Stewart, with front-man and vocalist Joe Retta being brought in to complete the line-up.

After an initial appearance on L.A. rock station 95.5 KLOS's popular 'Mark & Brian' radio program, the "Are You Ready Steve?" tour kicked off, at the Whisky a Go Go in Hollywood, on 12 June 2008. The band spent the next few months playing festivals and gigs throughout the U.S. and Canada, including Moondance Jam in Walker, Minnesota, having headlined at the Rock N Resort Music Festival in North Lawrence, Ohio, near Canal Fulton.

The tour also took in London, Ontario's Rock the Park, with another headlining gig at Peterborough's Festival of Lights, followed by the Common Ground Festival in Lansing, Michigan; then a benefit concert for victims of California's wildfires, at Qualcomm Stadium in San Diego, California.

In January 2009 the Sweet presented at the concert industry's Pollstar Awards, also having played a short set at the Nokia Theatre, where the event was held, marking the first time in the ceremony's history that a band had performed at the show. As well as local gigs at the House of Blues, on L.A.'s Sunset Strip and Universal CityWalk, 2009, the group returned to Canada for sold-out shows at the Mae Wilson Theater and Casino Regina, followed by the Nakusp Music Fest and Rockin' the Fields of Minnedosa, in Minnedosa, Manitoba. U.S. festivals also included Minnesota's Halfway Jam, Rockin' the Rivers in Montana, with Pat Travers and Peter Frampton, and two late-summer shows, at the Santa Cruz Beach Boardwalk.

The band recorded a cover version of the Beatles' "Ticket to Ride," which was included on Cleopatra Records' "Abbey Road," a Fab Four tribute CD that was released on 24 March 2009. A preview of the group's new CD "Live in America," which was recorded live at the Morongo Casino, Resort & Spa in Cabazon, California on 30 August 2008, was featured on KLOS's "Front Row" program on 12 April 2009. The CD, which was first sold at shows and via the band's on-line store, was released worldwide in an exclusive deal with Amazon.com, on 21 July 2009. The release received favourable reviews from The Rock n Roll Report, Classic Rock Revisited and Hard Rock Haven, among others.

In April 2010 the band released its first single on iTunes: an updated, hard rock version of the Beatles' "I Saw Her Standing There." Performances on the 2010 summer tour included the Wildflower! Arts and Music Festival in Richardson, Texas and Las Vegas, Nevada's Fremont Street Experience. Other concerts taken part in were Rock N' America in Oklahoma City, OK; Summer Jam in Des Moines, Iowa; Jack FM's Fifth Show at the Verizon Wireless Amphitheater in Los Angeles; an appearance at the Hard Rock Hotel in Biloxi, Mississippi; and the inaugural edition of the Thunder Mountain Rock Festival in Sawyer, North Dakota.

On 11 November 2010 it was announced that in May 2011 "Steve Priest's Sweet" had been booked to perform at a handful of European dates, but the gigs later had to be cancelled in late January 2011, after it was learned that one of the promoters was a suspected swindler, wanted by British law enforcement officials. As of February 2011, fans who purchased pre-sale tickets were still in the process of working through the administrative channels with PayPal and various banks and credit card issuers, to try to reclaim their money.

The group toured South America during March 2011 then were booked by a befriended female Belgian promoter, along with Journey, for two gigs in the east of Germany, on 27 and 28 May 2011, where in Borna and in Schwarzenberg, after more than 30 years away, Steve Priest got a warm welcome back in Europe.

On 12 August 2012, Stuart Smith resigned from his guitar duties, to dedicate more time to his "Heaven & Earth" project. Starting with the band's October 2012 appearance at the Festival Internacional Chihuahua in Mexico, Los Angeles-based guitarist Ricky Z. joined the group for their live performances then this lineup returned to Casino Regina in Saskatchewan, Canada in February 2013.

Tour dates played in summer 2013 included Riverfest in Watertown, Wisconsin, the St. Clair, MI Riverfest, several further dates in Canada, and a reprise of their appearances at both Moondance Jam in

Walker, MN and Rockin' the Rivers in Three Forks, Montana. The band made some rare appearances on the U.S. east coast in July 2013, including a performance with David Johansen of the New York Dolls at the Bergen Performing Arts Center in Englewood, New Jersey.

Their vocalist Joe Retta was unavailable for these dates due to a scheduling conflict, so Tribe of Gypsies frontman Chas West, who'd played with Jason Bonham's band and substituted in well-known bands including Foreigner, Lynch Mob and Diamond Head, stepped in for a series of shows in New York, New Jersey and Maryland.

On 27 August 2014, Steve Priest announced on the band's Facebook page that guitarist Mitch Perry had been recruited on guitar. Most recently on tour with Lita Ford, Mitch's other credentials included his work with Michael Schenker Group, Asia Featuring John Payne, Edgar Winter, Billy Sheehan and David Lee Roth. His first live appearance with Sweet was at the Rock the River festival in Saskatoon, Saskatchewan, on 23 August 2014.

On December 22, 2017 the 50th anniversary tour launched at the Whisky a Go Go, on L.A.'s Sunset Strip, with the introduction of new singer Paulie Z, a local musician known for hosting "Ultimate Jam Night." Z replaced Joe Retta, who'd been the frontman for the Los Angeles incarnation of Sweet since its formation in 2008.

Steve Priest was asked to join Tucker and Scott for their 1985 Australian tour, but declined at the last moment. Mike Chapman contacted Connolly, Priest, Scott, and Tucker in 1988, offering to finance a recording session in Los Angeles. As he remembered: "I met them at the airport and Andy and Mick came off the plane. I said, 'Where's Brian?' They said, 'Oh, he's coming.' All the people had come off the plane by now. Then this little old man hobbled towards us. He was shaking, and had a ghostly white face. I thought, 'Oh, Jesus Christ.' It was horrifying." Reworked studio versions of "Action" and "The Ballroom Blitz" were recorded, but it became clear that Connolly's voice and physical health had made Sweet's original member comeback too difficult to promote commercially, so the reunion attempt was aborted.

In 1990 this line-up was again reunited, for the promotion of a music documentary entitled Sweet's Ballroom Blitz. This UK video release, which contained UK TV performances from the 1970s and contemporary interviews, was released at Tower Records, London. Sweet members were interviewed by Power Hour, Super Channel, having spoken of a possible reunion.

Brian Connolly died at the age of 51 on February 9, 1997 from liver failure and repeated heart attacks, attributed to his abuse of alcohol in the 1970s and early 1980s. Mick Tucker subsequently died on February 14, 2002 from leukemia, at the age of 54.

Two versions of The Sweet are still active with original members: "Andy Scott's Sweet", which frequently tours across Europe as Sweet, with trips to other countries, including regular visits to Australia and "Steve Priest's Sweet," which tours the US and Canada.

On 28 April 2009, Shout! Factory released a two-disc, career-spanning greatest hits album, Action: The Sweet Anthology. It received a coveted four-star (out of five) rating in Rolling Stone magazine.

In an October 2012 appearance on Jimmy Kimmel Live, Axl Rose, lead singer of Guns N' Roses, referred to Sweet as having been one of his favourite bands when growing up, along with fellow British band Queen.

In April 2016, the chart topping song (1973), "The Ballroom Blitz" was featured in a trailer for Suicide Squad. In December 2016, their single "Fox on the Run" (1975) was featured in a trailer for Guardians of the Galaxy Vol. 2.

Band members

Classic lineup

Mick Tucker - drums, backing and lead vocals, percussion (1968–1981, 1985–1991)

Steve Priest - bass, backing and lead vocals (1968–1981)

Brian Connolly - lead vocals (1968–1979)

Andy Scott - guitars, backing and lead vocals, keyboards, synthesisers (1970–1982, 1985–1991)

Other members

Frank Torpey - guitars (1968–1969)

Mick Stewart - guitars (1969–1970)

Mal McNulty - bass, lead & backing vocals (1985–1991)

Paul Mario Day - lead vocals (1985–1989)

Phil Lanzon - keyboards, synthesisers, vocals (1985–1988)

Malcolm Pearson - keyboards, synthesisers (1988–1989)

Jeff Brown - bass, vocals (1989–1991)

Ian Gibbons - keyboards, synthesisers, vocals (1989)

Steve Mann - keyboards, synthesisers, vocals (1989–1991)

Touring musicians

Gary Moberley - keyboards, synthesizers (1978–1981)

Nico Ramsden - guitar (1978)

Ray McRiner - guitar (1979)

Discography

Funny How Sweet Co-Co Can Be (1971)

Sweet Fanny Adams (1974)

Desolation Boulevard (1974)

Give Us a Wink (1976)

Off the Record (1977)

Level Headed (1978)

Cut Above the Rest (1979)

Waters Edge (titled Sweet VI with a different cover in the U.S.) (1980)

Identity Crisis (1982)

Sweet

THE SWEET

40

Made in the USA
Las Vegas, NV
04 January 2022

40312298R00046